HOMUNCULUS

Luke Palmer is a prize-winning poet and critically acclaimed author. He lives in Wiltshire with his partner and their three daughters who, rightly, couldn't care less.

Also by Luke Palmer

Play	(Firefly Press, 2023)
Grow	(Firefly Press, 2021)
In all my books my father dies	(Red Ceilings Press, 2019)
Spring in the Hospital	(Prole Books, 2018)

ISBN: 978-1-915760-60-9

The author has asserted their right to be identified as the author of this Work in accordance with the Copyright, Designs and Patents Act 1988

Cover designed by Aaron Kent

Edited and Typeset by Aaron Kent

Broken Sleep Books Ltd
Rhydwen
Talgarreg
Ceredigion
SA44 4HB

Broken Sleep Books Ltd
Fair View
St Georges Road
Cornwall
PL26 7YH

Contents

Homunculus

Luke Palmer

Broken Sleep Books

Horse Mother

If [a human sperm] be fed wisely with the Arcanum of human blood,
and be nourished for up to forty weeks, and be kept in the even heat
of the horse's womb, a living human child grows therefrom.

— Paracelsus – De Natura Rerum (1537)

O great and latinate mother   there I was
haunched in your middle   mired inside
our bloody knot   plasma fattened
plump little barrel   the small bow
and tight stitch of   my shimmering
translucent brain

               I wanted to stay
squared in your uterus   womb-warm and duvet'd
galloped in your sternum   stuffed and packed
wanted to be kept   left to loll in your thick
limbic hedgerow   cooped in that belly
never to be dealt   but no

plans had been made   the world opened
so big my mother O

               so big and so so cold

Desire | Infant Mask

Sluggish with it | thick
in cheek and limb
with its going on | go on |
it's a brick | a thirst |
a lumbering forward | it's
a verb in the mouth | I want you
| put your verb in my mouth
and sink through it | I want
to sit at your feet | trace you
with my tongue | pick me
up | there's so much
I will take from you | I'm ripe
| doughy with need | and you
will want me | I'll suck your
want out of you | throw it
at a wall and watch
what happens when you
watch me do it | I'll swell
with it | this love

Homunculus in Ash

For it is to be known, that everything that is quickly or hastily made or born, doth soon perish.

— Paracelsus

Father lifts me   still warm to touch
my silver cratered skin   a wrinkled handkerchief
the moon in it   I am cut from tilled mist
from fire's spent fuel   whelped from the witherings

all night he was at it   working the furnace
flamebursts of wood   the coal's slow glow
he sprinkled with sand   drizzled with brine
to make perfect heat   and fix it in me

the sun sings mercurial   I feel it coursing
as my father peels a skein   from my rib
slips it under his tongue   and knows

Desire | Cleanliness

It gets me in the shower | mostly | but not like
that bit in *American Beauty* | where Lester's
jerking off | not like that | no | not at all | more
of an ache | the last thing I want is to be touched |
so it's a watch-the-droplets-on-the-shower-screen
sort of thing | an I-need-to-clean-that-limescale
kind of idle aching towards you | you
who have used this shower | and it's not
that I want to frame you in some sort of shower
of the mind | watch the water running down
your back | *cascading* the poet says | the black *cascade*
of your hair in the shower of my mind | it isn't | more
perhaps that the shower is a cleansing space | what I want
is the painful rush | the solar plexus opening
wide | the water getting right in | washing
it all out | doing it again | droplets of water
on my skin | my feet | and the puddles | so
many | many puddles

Homunculus, Potty Training

My father in his soiled apron
kneels to the rug I've soiled
sops it with caustic water
his cracked knuckles singing
so much soil and smut
while outside the earth stirs
the small machines rising
the shock of my own water
brings springs to my eyes and
father comforts me
says all water is blessed
is longing to fall
back to the centre and
the world's in endless gyre
around a hollow middle
where god sits and
he rises up through everything
muddied by what he touches
but still there inside
that seed spirit inherent
and I am a planet too
my divine core rising
to puddle on the kitchen floor
miraculous he says and smiles
his raw hands working the rug
beneath his knees and
my miraculous marks

Homunculus with Object Permanence

There are more nerves in my mouth
than in my hands

unless I hold the taste of things
they are taken from me

my mouth is loaded with tongue
I put my body in my mouth

to keep it safe
when I lie on my stomach

the world disappears
leaves only noise

sometimes my head opens
like a flower and sound spills out

the world's noises are fires
things seep from them

from the ash
I am learning

to recognise my father
I turn to his fire

and the world turns to smoke
I swallow it whole

Homunculus in Milk

Rimy slosh
around my nugget body
meniscus like a
second face I'm lost
beneath the surface
surprised to find inside
the bright slab darkness
wet and close lightless
and without margin
bubbles vanish
in the folds of it
here's one squeaking
from my mouth my
voice reaches the surface
cracks against air and
I'm lifted placed on a
block by the fire to dry
a thin sour sheen

A Discourse with Thirst

After Yinka Shonibare

Most days I still forget to drink;
once went a whole year without
then one morning — imagine —
woke up with a tap for a head.
I suppose it's funny in a way;
a fitting *Strewwelpeter* for our times.
No one notices as they once did the cut
of my jackets, my dry wit — why would they
when at my shoulders' confluence
is just this guttering spigot?

My new head pounds and I don't sleep well
— wake often to the drowned quiet
of the house. My wife left; felt wrong
to stay, she said. I talk to stones
until I've worn them right through
then hang them on a string around my neck.
It's hard to know why things happen.

Desire | Running

The newest of the fathers are running | stiff
from anxious worry and running | running
until the fleshy drum of themselves hits
target pace | running hearts pump in the fathers
each morning | they gather water in a sling and
start running | anywhere they can | launched
sweating into the suburbs | running away from
and then back to their homes | they run until
they are filled or emptied with running | in circles
incrementally wider | running until they can run
harder and longer and further | this is stamina |
all of the new fathers run after all of the past fathers
| it serves an evolutionary purpose | they can't
stop | they are peaking | full of pain | can't throw
their conditioning away | they'll lose it all | there
are programs to follow | tell them what they must do
but still they worry | they must stretch and warm
up | warm down | worry all those ligaments | always
under impact | so they run until they find the zone
| use their bodies | hit the wall | they run at night
or in the grey mornings | they run until they are
finished | blisters and children biting at their heels

Doomscrolling

Yes   today has been the bluntest
cross legged at the kitchen window
the same view pressing on it

the sills are deep with flies   ticking
consonants of small forms that
slowed against the glass then

shrunk   their cursive rasp
at my fingernails   only the fridge
hums now   meanwhile the sky

is faultless with swifts   I watch
vital parts of myself detach
lumber to the river where

they cease   I squeeze greenfly
from the bud of every rose
in all my prosperous beds

until my fingers change colour

Homunculus with Milk Tooth

All of the teeth that will ever be in my head
are in my head   lined up like slow cows
in pink flesh   improbable carillon

in my skull's belfry   where they wobble
and chime   dull   dull   each
little hammer   against my tongue

my gums are emptying   spat teeth
under my pillow   mouth full of
nothing   clammy wattles   spent

El Dorado

ride, boldly ride

Sometimes I don't recycle yoghurt pots. They fall
like fat rain to the wrong bin. Nice to know
there's a vessel condemned to outlast me — a totem
on the future's open plain. One day a cowboy
crosses a prairie, looks back. Does he see
the whole darned field or just the dark band
where his horse pushed through? Does he note
the scent rising from the grass, the shine
on his chaps? Later, when a lit Marlborough drops
from his square jaw, will he recognise his sore throat
and the valley ablaze behind him? I'm the cigarette
in this metaphor. What I'm trying to say is I'm
not sure who's seeker, who's sought, but the theme
plays out just the same.
Take me home. I'm the place you've arrived at.
There'll be no pushing on at this hour. There's wolves
in the hills. Can you hear them? Tomorrow, we'll ride
to the chilled goods aisle, pick whatever pudding you like.

Night Feed with Summer Solstice

Are they different, the winter's children?
Held tighter in the diurnal maw? Light
stirred less thick in the blood?

Two hours across the squandering dawn
I've tricked this ounce of milk to the small cave
in the pebble of your gut, and what luck
the day we're growing into

— the peach of it, the dove coo'd size of the thing
rearing up improbable as a giraffe's head
all eyes and wide cheeked in her stall.
Morning

and somewhere else night falls
on the other side of the year. Our days
lessen while theirs unfrond.
Things tip inevitably back to the centre

this room, the hour. Awake
my long breath in your ear calms you.
Yours is hot and short in mine.

Homunculus with Megalophobia

I am so very small
in the large world   trodden on
and skipping out from under
feet and heirlooms   there are weights
I'll never know   unliftable kernels
in other lives   their nuthouses
mine is spume   spindrift
spiderweb   wrens terrify me
the big slates of their eyes   even the air
seems bigger than I am   its little bubbles
finding their ways into my skin   sometimes
I think I might slip   in between things
blur into a margin   I rise on updrafts
from the kettle   find myself bedridden
in spells of dry weather   the air
holds down on me   I trundle up the green
ladders of the garden   quivering
in a daisy's penthouse   everywhere
is so far away   it feels made up
those clouds   for instance
what's a thing so heavy
doing   all the way up there

Inhale

late spring   I push elderflowers into my eyes
feed each petal clasp   its fuzzy stamen centrepiece
past the sealed rims   mucussed grip of conjunctiva
my palms smell of dog urine   a platinum sting
under fingernails as my eyes grow   globe   moon
a fizzy milk halo across walls   I blink creamy tears
hold them up to the light   gummy strands teased
between thumb and forefinger   clotted velvet
glistening
                               one night I cry
a sink full of green water   muddied with brackish rot
a head's worth of summer   pupils like fat berries'
unpicked ink falling from me   I bleed sight
like a scrag of fog peeled from a slow river   birds twitch
their hearts against bramble   jackdaws clumpy nests
hang in the corner of my mouth   I turn
to the earth   grope down to the blind roots
their white spools running from me   breath out

Desire | Grief

Dear | you disappear
| leave cups of tea
to mudden on the counter |
I cannot find you | when we
walk you're three steps on
and don't look back | this
isn't admonishment |
my hand in too-hot water
scares me | the scald's
gnaw | how it brings
comfort | I don't want to
live like this | this
stupor | a twisted thing
you drag around | half-
whelped carcass
coiled in the sheets
from our bed | Love |
the snake has you
on the river floor |
I'm on the bank | this
hooked line digs into
my palms | the pulse
along the wire is fading

Homunculus with Father-Rage

My father is sent a writ   his right to ride a horse
hereby rescinded   he's been reigned in
wrung from his stirrups   a stable is above his station
ripped from his grip   destabilised
he wreaks havoc in the house   flings tins at the walls
shouts from his shimmering messes   his diminished livery
so he leathers his filly on the high road   flails her flanks
and flogs her dead   outside the parish office
shows her bones to the councilmen   his dripping crop
cocked at her frothing eyes   her chewed off tongue
then he's done   prances off satisfied
the horse left cooling   in a pool of blood

Desire | Fathers

We threaten our daughters | hold them close
and threaten them | hold the threat
of a latex teat to their lips | they drink greedily |

we sing them to sleep | our threat songs | if they wake
we go to them | into their rooms | threaten them
with comfort | or lie with them | grip them tight

against us | our threat's breath mixes
with theirs | morning and they crawl to the lair
of our unmade beds | our bulk

threatens them | we doze a threatening doze
as they watch videos with no sound | we wash
their hair | we dress our threatened daughters | skirts

tights and neat shoes | in the park
they ride with threat on our backs | they fall
and hurt themselves | we put plasters on their torn skin |

sometimes we throw them over our heads | they laugh
until they cry | sometimes we threaten roughly | make them cry
and mean to | we feed them our threat | watch them

eat | we are so full of threat | our daughters
grow inside it | threat
follows our daughters | a daughter

in each fist | we do not want this | at night
we cross the street | not wanting the taught threat
of ourselves threatening the daughters | we announce

our threatening presence | our threat says | dear daughters
walk with fists full of keys | and if we come for you | no
matter what we look like | lock your doors fast against us

Homunculus at Play

We do the game
where you hit things with a stick
until they become something else

until the round things flatten
and the upright things flatten
and the hanging things fall

the crack of my switch, once
then a space springs up like god
all shiny and new

by the river
that shunts between banks
our sticks chip at its glossy top

for a glimpse
of muddy belly
wet sparks rain down

wind sharp in the trees
our feet
against the cold pebbles

Oubliette

Found one dull Sunday in a sunken corner
of a medieval theme park   drossed with filth
and a chocolate bar wrapper they don't sell anymore
   small change silvers the flagstones
   where someone's sought luck or
    bought off thoughts of this most human mouth and godless throat
     thoughts that corpses flooded the waiting corpses
     thoughts of disappearance   a slow unlearning of parts
     parts they hadn't even named back then
        no word yet for duodenum puckered like saltfish
        no word yet for medulla oblongata
        ticking in the lizard dark
           as the damned count back on each tripartite finger
           the tongue's loose meat gone bad   O machine
           of silences how should I pay to forget?

Cruelty

You wonder how long this can go on
— Raymond Carver

Part of you meant it   the trowel born down
the pink flesh twiced   dancing
and you'd rather be honest than liked
so tell the full two minutes of this earthworm
turning its axis   the coil of it jolted
by its snipped wrecked midriff as   further back
float the shrews you drowned in the canal
who bit down on their last breaths then burst
far off in dark water   up pops the rabbit
a mess of undergrowth by the time you'd done
its kinked neck uprooted   eyes bulbed
as you went again with the axe and then
     last week   the mauve-purple bloom
of a rats' nest mewling on your shovel
eight or nine blunt young at two days old
and useless   barely limbed and slow
through the parted warmth of the compost bin
these little rot-blossoms dragged themselves
as you wondered how to do it — a quick nick
with a blade to empty them like thumbs   or
a bucket   their dumbness shushed
in the end you couldn't stomach it
left them squeaking like saws trying to crawl
back to the warm earth   back to their mother
who won't come for them anyway
and she likely dugged with new litter so there
they lay alone   small marrow of small bones
leeching to subsoil   now the worm slows
you nudge it to a hole
press down the root ball of next year's crop

Desire | Winter

After Stan Brakhage

If you were a dog | and dead | I would
lay you out to rot beneath a tree | but you'd not
rot | you'd freeze | white petal-bloom
along your flank | gums frost burned
from your teeth | eyelids gone | a startled
look | lying there while the ground
refused you | your own shell hard
around your heart's red rock

you'd shrink with the thaw | rains
would fall and blacken you | slake you
to the soil | in the gaps | spurts of nettle
and primrose | one night a wild thing
would nose you | drag you off | there'd be
tracks where your bare ribs clung | churned
brown earth | nothing left to mourn
before the spring

Houseplants

All the houseplants are dying   the nub
of each leaf gummy with floss   a bitter smell
to the sap   sharp and fox-like in the back
of the throat   they have turned

from the light   drawn up like old spiders
no doubt its treatable   but I haven't
strength left   tip tea dregs on dead leaves
crisping in the pots   something's burrowing

in one dusty bowl   soil blown thin
all its stores leached out   just a matter
of time now   while other matters
thump through the walls   their mustered ranks

like a still life   like fruit caught
on the shrivelling turn   or empty rooms
that aren't really empty   like something ticking
at the edges   so sure of itself

Homunculus with Life Power

The alchemist grows and cooks in the stomach
— Paracelsus – Volumen Paramirum (1575)

my father has eaten bad meat but
there's a man in his stomach who knows
how to trim malchop from good
how to chop rich meat from poor
my father is a poorly man
sprawled on his bed
trussed in a fever
he trusts me to feed him
bread soaked in ewe's milk
both things being born of grass
my father needs rooting he says
and the milk grass and the bread grass
go to work in him
he settles
his breathing easing
I perch on his chest
watch the sweat dry
the salt come to his hairline
his eyes lined and puffed
with yeasty bags under them
I take raw meat and
place it on his eyes
to draw the salt out
the grass he has eaten
distilled through his flesh
into this flesh I'll bury in the garden
where the grains grow and the sheep eat

Homunculus and Bird

I lie quite a lot   put things together that
weren't together   there's fallacy everywhere

once I found a blackbird   not quite dead
under the kitchen window   I picked him up

felt his fizzy heart   his ticky feathers
and put him in a shoebox   to sleep it off

and soon I heard him   the scratchy birdy
so I dug him a worm   squished it a bit first

but he wouldn't eat   there was mess in his box
his claws had drawn in it   I left the lid off

my bird just sat there   evening coming on
then another blackbird came   and killed him

beak like a needle   dragged him over the fence
in a puff of grey feathers   nothing left

words let you make lines   a kind of order
between things   but it's all made up

you keep going don't you   you keep
smiling don't you   until *the end*

You wake because an elephant hawkmoth

very very slowly
is the image of a bridge
brought and coloured
until it glows
greenly pink / pinkly
green   also
is a sound bright &
very very
close until you could almost
write on it
so big in the scale
of small things so
bigly small this thing
plapped   plapping
on the lampshade   an
umbrella opened indoors
a car in a shopping centre
a house built inside
a slightly larger house
inside a country chapel

Desire | Dad Bod

Put you in my house
— John Lee Hooker

Tonight I found my collarbone's drum note | a sharp
tap and it throats like a tom tom | the sternum drops
an octave | some gap perhaps | behind the lung
| an intercostal misstep | makes thunder | if you like
I'll play myself for you | one evening when
our blood's up | our daughters quiet or asleep |
our daughters who don't know their separate
bodies' borders | still too young | they share selflessly |
what age does the body become something else | synonym
like it is for us grown-ups | isn't it | tell me | when I give you
this | my body | when I talk my body to you | whisper it
to your eager ear | am I saying my body as it is | is it this body
that reaches you when I give you my body to hold | how much
arrives of what falls through the world | observable
at the mirror | its foul audience | things bubble up | bad end
of a hair follicle | ingrown and coaxed with tweezers | red swell
at the jaw's thin flesh | when you see me look at you
do you clock the splodge on my eyeball | an egg
gone over | or my narrow bridge | oily T zone | if I eat
too much sugar it all peels | I'm not attached to it | this body's
reluctant tenant | these hairy allotments | but you place it
in your hands | clutch it | say you like some parts
like the thighs | one's scarred from a football stud
caught at twelve years old | three-inch ragged ladder
your fingers climb | time piece | shiny cicatrix |
there's another nick inside the wrist | site of a bone-pin
after I broke it drinking whisky at fifteen | a tiny star
fresh when we met | remember | this body at sixteen |
puppy fat balled on its smooth chest | once

struck a hardware salesman dumb | I asked
for a box of fifty mil countersunk | got ogled
in the warehouse | my hair gold and long
| I was called out in toilet queues | *we think you have*
the wrong line | *miss* | why am I saying
this | as point of departure | to show this body
has lied before | that people can be wrong |
but tonight I found my collarbone's drum note | play it
and the soft mammal opens up | is coaxed
to a run | shhhh | our daughters are sleeping | my hollow body
goes boom boom boom boom | ahaw haw haw haw

Homunculus with Invoked Father

I ask my father   who is my father
his cricked neck tilts back   falls again
to find me in his books   *little godspawn*

he whispers   *there is fire*
in you   let us work to get at it
may all our fathers be merciful   later

he's tupping the maid   I watch
from a keyhole   his bare arse at her back
I slip into the woodwork   my father rises

empties his bladder   then spits
we're the same you and I   just as immaculate
he goes on   across the fields

Hansel

A father is a god who won't feed you
who lolls in bed on heat his new wife stewing
in him, bindweed in his knotty body, his bark
coarse and pitted as your unmother
pulls at your sister's hair, tells you
what all boys are like. A father
is a god of stale bread clutched to your chest
as you follow him into the woods. He makes
you a fire, a lazy red mouth
says to keep it fed
while he works.
                A father speaks like a steady axe.
He speaks to you long after he has left his axe
tied to a branch spinning in the wind. He echoes
long after you find his aeolian drum, claw at it
and break it with aching fingernails for your father
is a god in the wind. You creep back to his fire
your sister choking on bread and tears. There is smoke
in your eyes and a whole forest
to burn while you wait
for him.

                Years later you will remember
as you clear the breakfast dishes, as the sink fills
and you tip cereal to the bin. Upstairs, your daughters
will play, cry from your bed, squealing in duvets,
buried in pillows. You will brave the knives
in the draining rack and remember that you
could be a god like this. Your god will hang
over you in the playroom as you scoop up blocks
lay dolls in their crib stack books on their shelves.

Your god is a father
who whispers.

A father is a forest
row on row of trees all ways even and uniform
and dark. You try to cross a father, trip
on his creeping knuckles, fall to his knees.
A net of branches forms a father so dense you forget
the real sky as a father paws at your sister's hair.
Dark water is a father falling through the canopy.
A father drips down your neck. In places a father
lies so thick you must wade through
up to your waist.
When you wake
lost in a father you forget the way you came
and set off again still hungry, always hungry.
There is sap on your hands its smell sharp
and fleeting like smoke. Your clothes cling
to you dark and cold as you set off again
even deeper as the lightless water
drips and keeps dripping
in the empty
father.

You will remember this
years later as you get your daughters ready,
roll thick tights up their legs, lift them
by the waist. You will remember this as you
plump their arms into vests dresses jumpers
as you pack their lunchboxes as they pin
each other's hair in the way you showed them
the sharp clasp at the nape of their necks.
The father outside your window
taps his nails on the glass
creaks in the wind.

At the centre of the forest
a father rests you in his generous house. His arms
swing open and his sky rises up up up until it winks
and dances in greenlight a great lime-leaf firmament
and roof of young beech. It stretches under the earth.
A father's walls are fruiting with oysters, parasols
spring like footstools, chantarelles in fountains
across the floor. A father frames his windows
with sorrel and mustard, goatsbeard and brooklime
and smock. A father's kitchen is a stream-bed of crayfish.
You grow inside this father, fill
to your edges, brim to your
blistering waistband.
                                    But there's a tug
your body's cage tightening. The air turns turgid.
You sleep beside your rounding sister, sweating
dreams of your father who led you to the woods
of the woman who led your father up your father's stairs.
Your father is a forest pushing blood through you
like sap sweetening in the trunks
frogs bulbed in the ponds
knotted with a simple
pulse calling you
home.

        As you, years later, wring your daughter's
socks, churn them in hot water, your hands chafing
in the cold air, you will remember that walk home.
You will remember as you watch socks dancing
lines across your father's garden
where the swingset you made
holds the forest back.

Your father waited
in his woodsman's house that dawn, his axe like a limb
in the porch-post. Your father met you at his door
glowing. An earthy scent trailed him. Surprise
in your father's face as if he'd never met you
you plum from the woods and your sister bittered
tree-scratched swollen out of herself with bitterness
as you took in your father
his open shirt.

           Inside the smell was stronger
among the clothes, gauze, lace, such small pieces.
Your stepmother dripped down the stairs
uncoiled on the couch.

                      Gretel left,
tends bars now in some logging town. But you stayed
snared by how it might taste, might coat the tongue
like gingerbread. Your father steered you
to the forest then, said you'd earned
your axe, would help you
pray with it

And now, this years-later morning, your father
      at the treeline, his blade head caught
    in the sun. You load the wagon's ropes,
      pulleys, oil and whetstone and bread.
      Your daughters run ahead laughing
        run through him like dust motes
         in and out of him as he walks
           as if he wasn't there
            as if he was just
              the forest
               .

They run in and out of his mouth.

Homunculus with Tree

*man may be compared to a tree, drawing his nutriment from the
earth, and from the surrounding air*
— Paracelsus

Trees will take anything inside them
iron railings barbed wire   God
rarely interferes though the trees shake
their knotty fists at Him   plant a man

right and he'll live six months in the earth
before the devil takes him
some forests are full of angry corpses
groaning away their last psalms

the rising sun on their faces   their lips
like leaves   flip a tree on its crown
and its roots are a dark mirror   as above
so below   it's the same with a man

below the knee is where the devil gets in
slinking through the xylem   you pick up
the devil just walking along   each step
unctuous   mud farting at your heels

all that blood and excrement you've shed
since you were a nut in your mother's womb
so   you walk under trees in winter
feel better   their blood marred

as yours is   those bare fingers
pointing out the blame   up there
over here   and there
and here

Impotent

They've changed the shape of bank notes
and there's no one on TV anymore
I recognise. I've affected a limp

but still it's the little things
that lodge like lint or hair under the fridge
clogging up the mechanism. If I could just

open up the way a coffeeshop is open.
Or maybe it's a door. Meanwhile
there's a flow of things that must be worn

they say, shrugged on like clothes
or new shoes kicked into shape. It must
be worn the way that hair is worn

nowadays. Like a simile.
I have lost the smell of my own dust,
my knees ache, and the rain —

the rain's intimate monologue rolls out
through the trees   so quietly.

Homunculus with Birthday Party

Knee slides across the village hall   my shirt
crackles static as I spin   we are all so positively
charged   the air is dry and thin

my father wears a pointy hat   the elastic's
cinching his chin   he takes four strides
to the middle of the room   he raises his arms

in the din *it's a game*   he shouts
called wobbly alchemist   the children follow him
the web of infants tightens   things speed up

I watch and don't join in   a fist rings his every finger
two torsos lock on to each shin   someone's mounting
his toppled back   a victory flag for a grin

then I'm into them all and flailing
at their intruder abdomens   punching their cuckoo guts
choked on cake and rage   a taste like iron

and tin   until I'm father-handled into a back room
where he tends my injured skin   it's just a game
he says breathe out   breathe in

we open the gifts when the guests are gone
I tear at the paper and string   inside each box
nests a nugget of gold   big as a severed limb

Homunculus pokes himself in the eye

Man schliesse darauf die Offnung
— Goethe – Theory of Colours (1810)

Behind my shut lid a bright sear   pixel-glut green shuddering
of spilled white waves   red rust in an ochre halo
whorled storm of the eyeball   seeps all the way down
the bottom corner's murky river   pulsing swell of manycolour
shoots across in glaucous rolls   lime-blanched with welts
of lilac fire in a fish lens   a slant horizon
all beaks and claws   my iris bolting cyan
roil of milky frog-cloud   until the bruise-tongue gives way
cracks a stick of yellow   throbs an orange checker-plate
fluid's final judderings   as the organ finds its edge
but doesn't open

                 slowly

                       in the middle
grey against slow lightening   glutinously forming
my inner eye strains indefinitely   towards a path of stones

May
2019

The children are so pretty in their grief.
They hold it — a coltish thing on a short rope.
Their hands burn with its holding.

They have laid their flowers under a tree
and listen hard to a silence that is wind,
all children together

in a rough circle. The silence
is whole though it is not wholly silent.
The children are a flicker of cellophane.

Above the children, a white line appears
against the blue. They do not notice.
More arrive.

They join hands and wait
in the soft afternoon. And grief idles
so prettily in the children.

Desire | Ornithology

This one is a skilled fisher | watch
him dip to the river's lips | pluck a digit
writhing | the river moans | our lens
is long | it brings him to us | drops him
at the end of our nose | observe
the glaze on each feather | the oil
sheen across his back | look
at the span of him | all that flexion | taught
skin prickled with flight | almost
can you smell him | can you | say
his name | your throat holds it | how could you
not want to | bring him down | sink your bolt
right through him | watch all that life take
to the air | do it now | see he drops again
to the river | as if his tongue | shot
from his mouth | goes on at lapping | lapping

Meatspace

Summer   the same long day eeking out
commit everything to its little frame
like a lepidopterist   take care

don't smudge the summer's wings
or scuzz its furry abdomen
sometimes rain is just a noise   a pack

of flies at their articles   unpicks itself
until it smithereens in the puddles
a panic of peg dolls   their wet round heads gulp

push sand around the house   let it build
in the corners 'til you shake it out
down the gutters   no *you're* raining

and the beach a stuffed mouth at dusk
clouds over it the colour of pulpy corpses
there's dolphins in the bay   maybe a seal

you want to throw a mug against the wall

Homunculus with Wasp

Nature also forges man, now a gold man, now a silver man, now a fig
man, now a bean man.

— Paracelsus – Four Treatises (1538)

there's a wasp   visits the windowpane
a perfect shiny head   geared like a ratchet
fat jaws at the sash   as I watch it
loosening wood

            back at the nest
a papery ball   it spits out the pulp

        wood   translated

           what wood stays
in the wasp   knotted in the thorax
fine grained abdomen   does it know its home
was a window   does it recall my face
a blurry ghost   as I sit at the glass

regurgitate this nest   from words
watching the wasp   as it dreams

Desire | Leisure Centre

O | men of the swimming pool changing room | give me
your panting | wet breath charged with your lungs' blood
| that has kissed your heart through a gauze | thin
as a wedding veil | you fresh from the pool | marshalling
your clouds of spent air | let me gather them | such exhalations
your vocal chords sing | the *uh* of labour | the *uh*
of investment | and you in the shower | slick and whistling
your hot and coursing life | whistle to me | I will stitch it
with these others | men of the swimming pool changing room
permit me | I shall wear your panting | a garment
of sighs | beneath this hasty workshirt | warm | it shall cover me
tonight | by morning they shall mist my window | these tiny beads
you have laced me with | and I thank you | I thank you

You shouldn't start with the weather

but the rain was significant
the first rainfall of note that year
the country had been crying out for it
and gladly received each silver lance
in quiet supplication   the only noise
being soft and insistent rain
manholes chundered fatly
pavements ran with it   they ran so fast
as to almost take off   we stayed inside
looking out of windows obscured
with dribbling pellets of water so clear
it looked like nodules of glass on the glass
all bothering and jostling over each other
like translucent beetles or shimmering amoeba
in fact if you zoomed out far enough
the whole map was just one single
organism   the rain's plump foot
flat and viscous   its blurred body
plugged straight into the clouds
and us beneath it all
staggered and awestruck
while the sky continued on its blue way
somewhere up there and very far out

Homunculus at the Soft Play

There are worse things mouths my father
clasping lukewarm coffee to his chest.

He follows me through the ball pit
with his eyes. I can't breathe in here

and it smells like other people's spit.
I climb. I wave down at him

from the tallest tower. There is a new
coffee stain on his shirt. Sweat prickles

my back and my fingers grip the netting
like pudgy talons. He is talking

to another father. *There are worse things*
he says again *than loving a child*.

All My Friends Are Coupling-Up

I have a pet flood.
It lives in the yard — a throat
of rising water

that hums when it's stroked
that waits up for me
and has no truck with strangers.

I step into it — slough clothes
have rings ripped tenderly
from my fingers. I empty it

below the cliffs — a spill
of accoutrements
picked clean by gulls.

It is good to have a pet flood.
It will eat whatever you feed it.
In many ways it is predictable

but it's not the kind of pet
to hold to your chest
or turn your back on.

Desire | Cute

after Rachel McLean's Eyes To Me

O clutchable thing | sit in my
pocket | hair neat as a shop
over your ears all shiny like frost
with newness | your pearl-handled
pistols | your holster leather glossed
from the abattoir | just to hold
you | thumb and forefinger | squish
it up and slurp the pulp | no sweat
no whiskers | chubby forever | oh
what ears | what teeth | I'd give my eye
tooth to bring you to market | bleat
for me | factory fresh smell
like a new body | heart a frothy
bauble oh | taught as a drumskin | wax
-work no entry sign | in my fist | on my
lap | eyes like glass drips with eyes
painted on them | couldn't you just

Homunculus with Blood

After anything protracted   an ache will come
starting in a joint   some softer portion
sometimes there's blood   on the outside blood
where it shouldn't be   blood is the body's word
bruising the surface   with correction

what happens   when things from outside
get where they shouldn't   outside words
will bleed into me   resolved like a poem
before I write it down   did the world stop
looking as it did   it is very different now

Desire | Foraging

Honey fungus | sweet as death they tongue
from stumps | squat under dirty groundcover |
like rain-soaked skin mags older boys would show you
| unidentified specimens | leering boys | all gang
and posture | who smoked inexpertly | clucked
at the torn pages | the strange chimera | glands
| fruitbodies | all glisten | rotten sex | boys who watched
your face snare as the world grew suddenly
more | lesser than it was before | boys with mothers
already ruined | a look you couldn't place | but
shared | tried to ape | spent teenage years
kicking every bush | wanting more | until
you'd spot at twenty yards the first glint
of gloss smuggled under branches | do things
change | you seek other matter | these gummy tufts
the book describes | pullulate | its says | are they trussed
in smutty fishnet rhizomes | saprobial beneath dead bark |
you pluck a few | take them home to cook | place
their sweetmeats delicately | in your mouth

Jesus in the Networked Battlespace

It's not difficult   forgiveness

but must be absolute   everywhere at once
like the first swell of light
from a bomb   like my name

There is no carriage here   no
chassis   And red flowers
do not grow

in the temperature-controlled server rooms
of idolatry   O

what's weight to the weightless

This blood is not real   it washes
easily enough

Homunculus with Azoth of the Red Lion

it started in her liver
so my father salved
her slippery organ
with his cup of rust

filled her belly with angels
and she rose   took three steps
then threw herself at his feet
my father made a girl

walk again
rewrote her bones
with his inky tincture
and I watched him

pomped on his horsetop
the wine they gifted him
burned in his cheeks
as we left town

it's a choice
to remain hopeful

three days later
and the letter reached us
somewhere else

the girl had died
still
the girl's mother
sent her thanks

said her daughter
had never been
so much
herself

Dogs

for Tim Liardet

I walk mine through the spoil ponds and slag
of the housing estate, stutters of frost on the path,

mud's knuckle between them.
The sky's vault is a flat grey lowering.

Marsh grass capped in ice chitters
like a cold joint. News from last week

— two mastiffs parting a small-breed,
the mutt from next door jawed by a bloodhound —

has me rattled. And there's more people crushed,
left bloody and soft by livestock; their dogs run off

to shiver in the underbrush as the cows' heads
dip, the hooves come in. Even a un-grown bullock

weighs half a tonne. Who knows what starts them.
I stop, reel my dog back to its lead, turn for home.

As we re-climb the hill our breaths smoke.

Homunculus with Pot Boiler

The world is built from the morpheme up. I write
the flowers die and the flowers die. Tonight
I pin a wasp between my thumb and finger.
It leaves a three-inch barb in my palm.
The end unfurls like feathers.

There's a shift in the trees. The whole arboretum shakes.
I don't know who died and made me caretaker
but I can't perform my checks of these
long abandoned buildings
without creeping terror rising in me.

I did see someone now you come to mention it
a few miles back in my rear view mirror.
I'm overthinking this. Keep the locks
well oiled. There is a hole in the roof
and the drips ache and ache and ache and

Desire | Freud

In the dream | when I show the doctor my penis she stares | non-plussed | *what's the problem here exactly* | it's not supposed to be like that | *nothing is supposed to be like that* | we both stare | it's forked | a sausagey 'Y' | pink in my palm like a mouseling | *it looks fine very healthy* | she prods it with the blunt end of a pencil | tilts her head | it springs back | its doughy velum blushing | *like a plump ripe fruit* | two hooded snouts | it's well weighted | hangs in my palm like a warm bath | *a well-kept specimen* | I ask about the plumbing | *there's really very little we can do* [beat] *is there any pain* | quite the contrary | a weak laugh | she pats it | *well we can put you away now* | taking off her glove steering me to the door | it's warm outside | I whistle a tune | look at clouds | book a follow-up appointment

Homunculus as Misread First Line

After Sophie Collins

I am first encountered as a scaffold
runged up against the debilitate wall
of a rundown institution   an orphanage
likely being converted to flats
that will without irony prove too small
for families   where was I   I am seen
as a stiff rigged trellis of planks
and steel like a corset   stepped
like gallows with a ladder
inside of me and a thin gauze like skin
stapled around the outside
of me   what was I saying   I am subject
to the demonstrative acts
of louder men whose calloused hands
work to loosen joints   limbs   nuts
slung in the back of a lorry
and also to rusting
what am I doing   I succeed at
the girdered interface of the built
and the not-ready-yet   flat pack tower
many legged platform   untree   dead
and voiceless   voiceless O
O again   what is it all for

Desire | Sea

Who'd deny | a thing that vast
ululating | so steeped in edge and surface | palm
on the land's foot | we come
to the assertion of salt | each wave's shut lock
collapsing | a thrash of bolts
writhing | and at night
in the darkness | down there alone
continuing | I will come to you | nothing
on my feet | surround me | take me down | your
fruit de mer dressed in wrack | no skin
but all skin | no muscle
but all muscle | collapse me
with your rough blade down my throat | saddle me
in your hammock | recall me
to the pink canal of the conch shell | the brine
whispering | your wet sheets | shifting bed
full of horses | all the spume in the world

Homunculus by the Shore

at the tideline with my father   we are the only uprights
sea skidding white fur up the strand   sea always arriving
coming to me and arriving at me   like an eager dog
bringing all its versions   the rotten smell of itself

my father digs with his big toe   *the sea goes through that*
he says *waves don't break*   *they go down*
the hill of the sea is inside out   *waves roll up it*
all the way to the top   they end at my feet

my father swings me   high over the waves
that go down forever   down to the sea's throat
belching out water   *the sea is a generous element*
it will hold you up   *it will let you in*

he plants my feet in the water   the water sucks at them
like a hungry tongue   I'm brought to the edge
teetering in two places at once   against the flat world
wind stings the line of my lips   salt in the corners of my feet

Homunculus with Father-Eunuch

After Robert Hass

He's wrapped a wax strip round his crotch
fashioned a stump   a tallow goitre
that bulbs in his breeches

his balls were took   he says
by a wild boar   or a young bull
or three apothecaries   their rusty knives

the myriad construals
of my father's family jewels

it's all bollocks   if you ask me
but he prattles on   turgid with mercury
his own stock   off his nut

that boar   he roars
gored my loins   his horny tooth
my split purse   I trailed tubes
both pearls   gone for sweetmeats

like there is no other care
but les testicules de mon père

the bull   he fumes
who pronged my dong   who tilted my point
pierced my prick   like an egg
blown   under a mason's hammer

that's where all the woe is
in my father's popped cajónes

the reek of booze   he rues
on their breath   as they flayed me
at your grandpa's table   their sport
my arms pinned   to nip me in the bud

it's all he talks about
but his spuds still spat me out

Homunculus with Thresholds

my father crawls   stops and crawls again

stops in doorways   tracks the flagpole's shadow

around the town square   tucks his legs up

when a cloud passes   won't move past

holly on the greenway   must be dragged

over crazy paving   he's trying to prove something

has made his bed a tent   won't have his skin

touch eiderdown   lest his skin should grow

feathered he says   he breathes through parchment

won't have the fire's smuts write in him   he says

must keep his lungs clean   in fact

if you look close enough   there's no telling

where my father ends   and air begins

he barely moves   as the world advances

my father   shrinks

Homunculus with Brother

Eins andern knecht soll nieman seyn der fur sich bleyben kann alleyn
— Motto of Paracelsus

it was a fake brother   it was a shadow brother
it was a brother   made up for convenience
it was a fled brother   a brother that abandoned
its brother   it was someone else's brother
only a fleeting resemblance   something
in the teeth   it was a brother in the night
in the land   in a boat with many other brothers
it was on the wind my brother   in the rain
that fell on the sea   it was not always
my brother   we cast him from sand
on a family holiday   see my brother's feet
are smaller than mine   he lives a long way
from here   my brother answers the phone
using my voice   my brother doesn't pick up
he was the brother I wanted to be   he didn't exist
my brother crossed the world   my brother returned
he came up behind me   he held my other hand

Homunculus with Sulphur of Father

My father won't move his jaw for fear
of it falling out   sits hunched
by the fire   shaking and steaming

and shaking   he is a cloud
on the inside   parts of him silvered
and quick as mist

now he has begun
to snow   dusting his workshop
with fine silt   a thin dawn

across his vials of other weather
a sound moves from his little lips
like something melting

Desire | Youth

Carefully | so carefully because you have already
stepped | will at some point step | from a warm interior
into a blustery courtyard | at the precise moment
a gust of wind whipped | in the instant the wind will
whip your hair around your tender head | and the person who
walked | the person who will walk | with you through
that door | whose long hair also flew | whose hair will also
in that gust of wind mingle with your own | some of it
almost entering you | completing you in that moment | and
because you saw | you will come to see | that something
for a second just beyond your grasp | came like a kitten
to your fingers | comes almost close enough before | it was
called away | it will be called away in the very gust that will
bring it to you | in the same gust that brought it | and because
you knew all this that October morning | one October morning
you will witness from an upstairs window | as two people step
into a gust of wind | maybe years later | all those years gone by
might make its passing easier | this will be the hardest thing to bear

Homunculus on the Ring Road

[The Philosopher's Stone] purifies the body of all its natural filth ... so that no fault remains in it.

— Paracelsus, Opera Omnia (1589-91)

I trudge along the wet verge   grey sluice
of wheels on tarmac   roadside sod like little skulls
and Daddy in a bin bag   hauled behind me

I'm harnessed up   the poor and horse-born son
forced to shlep his dead dad   he bleats and whines
but won't die   before I die

though his brain's passed through his ears   no matter
his lips are chapped to bone   the gristle
that stitched him's all undone   still he croaks on

mile after difficult mile   until the bag splits
and he's disinterred at a truck stop   one foot
slithers to a kerb   it's years since I've seen him like this

in the open   there's a green sheen to him now
and something's in his fist   I loosen his grip
tease a wad of cloth from its fleshy nest

a stone slips out   his tongueless gob widens
forms a smile   on the tarmac lies a pocked and rimy moon
the source of his life's sauce   I pick it up
turn it in my magic hand   my father laughs

Outro

My children are a long way from me
across the beach, only blue sky beyond them.

Sunlight cuts them out flawlessly
above the sand. One child lies on their stomach

as the other bends. Together they are
the size of a cloud, many miles across

or maybe more and so high
that I am a teetering speck

on the edge of their world.
Each of these grains of sand

might have been another father
walking towards them

spreading their arms
to an open blue future.

The dunes tip towards the sea.
Now my children are swimming.

One waits. The other catches up. They dive
beneath the waves and do not look back.

Acknowledgements

I am grateful to the editors of the following journals in which some of these poems, in various forms, first appeared: *Anthropocene, Babel Tower Notice Board, Iamb, Ink Sweat & Tears, The Interpreter's House, Lighthouse, Poetry Birmingham, Poetry Wales, Raceme, the Scores, Under the Radar.*

'Desire | Fathers' won the Winchester Poetry Prize, 2022. Thanks to Jo Bell. 'Cruelty' came second in the Verve Poetry Contest, 2022. Thanks to Caroline Bird. 'Hansel' was commissioned for the podcast *Bedtime Stories for the End of the World*. Thanks to Eleanor Penny, Tom MacAndrew and Joe Dunthorne. 'Homonculus with Tree' was commended in the Ambit 'Magick' contest 2023. Thanks to Rebecca Tamás. 'Desire | Youth' came third in the Winchester Poetry Prize, 2021. Thanks to Andrew McMillan

The following books were invaluable in providing some insight into the life of Paracelsus (c.1493-1541) whose concept of the homunculus was the jumping off point for this collection.
- Philip Ball, *The Devil's Doctor* (2007)
- Franz Hartmann, *The Life & Teachings of Paracelsus* (1887)
- Henry M. Pachter, *Paracelsus: Magic into Science* (1951)
- Paracelsus, *Of the Supreme Mysteries of Nature* (trans. R Turner, 1656)

A big thank you to everyone who has offered advice and guidance on these poems and all things poetry-related. Particular thanks to Vik Shirley, Tim Liardet, Carrie Etter, Sean Borodale, Caleb Parkin and the HOURS writers. And to Aaron Kent for bringing this book into the world.

Finally, to my family, everything.

LAY OUT YOUR UNREST

Milton Keynes UK
Ingram Content Group UK Ltd.
UKHW010615160124
436115UK00003B/31

9 781915 760609